W9-BIR-829

Kid Pick!

Title: _____

Author: _____ 32609

Picked by: _____

_____

Why I love this book:

_____

_____

Profiles in Greek and Roman Mythology

ODYSSEUS

Mitchell Lane
PUBLISHERS

P.O. Box 196
Hockessin, Delaware 19707
Visit us on the web: www.mitchelllane.com
Comments? email us: mitchelllane@mitchelllane.com

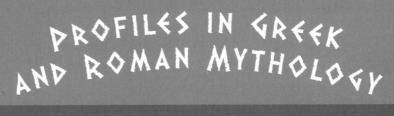

PROFILES IN GREEK AND ROMAN MYTHOLOGY

Titles in the Series

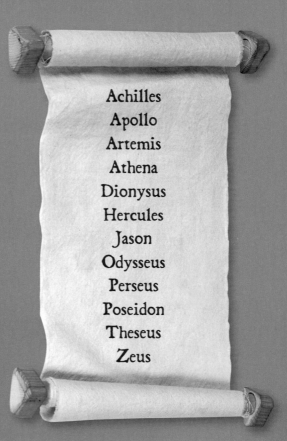

Profiles in Greek and Roman Mythology

ODYSSEUS

Kathleen Tracy

Mitchell Lane
PUBLISHERS

P.O. Box 196
Hockessin, Delaware 19707
Visit us on the web: www.mitchelllane.com
Comments? email us: mitchelllane@mitchelllane.com

Printing   1   2   3   4   5   6   7   8   9

Library of Congress Cataloging-in-Publication Data
Tracy, Kathleen.
   Odysseus / by Kathleen Tracy.
      p. cm. — (Profiles in Greek and Roman mythology)
   Includes bibliographical references and index.
   ISBN 978-1-58415-705-2 (library bound)
   1. Odysseus (Greek mythology)—Juvenile literature. 2. Trojan War—Juvenile literature.
I. Title.
   BL820.O3T73 2009
   398.20938'02—dc22
                                                                        2008020915

ABOUT THE AUTHOR: Kathleen Tracy has been a journalist for over twenty years. Her writing has been featured in magazines including *The Toronto Star*'s "Star Week," *A&E Biography* magazine, *KidScreen* and *TV Times*. She is also the author of numerous books for Mitchell Lane Publishers, including *William Hewlett: Pioneer of the Computer Age; The Fall of the Berlin Wall; Leonardo da Vinci; The Story of September 11, 2001; Johnny Depp; Mariah Carey;* and *Kelly Clarkson.*

PUBLISHER'S NOTE: This story is based on the author's extensive research, which she believes to be accurate. Documentation of such research is contained on page 46.

The internet sites referenced herein were active as of the publication date. Due to the fleeting nature of some web sites, we cannot guarantee they will all be active when you are reading this book.

To reflect current usage, we have chosen to use the secular era designations BCE ("before the common era") and CE ("of the common era") instead of the traditional designations BC ("before Christ") and AD (*anno Domini,* "in the year of the Lord").

TABLE OF CONTENTS

Profiles in Greek and Roman Mythology

The Trojans discuss whether to believe a large wooden horse left outside their city gates is truly a gift from the goddess Athena. Little do they know it is a clever carrier for Greek soldiers, devised by the cunning Odysseus.

ODYSSEUS

CHAPTER 1

Beware of Greeks Bearing Gifts

For ten years the Greeks had besieged the city of Troy and battled the towns in Troy's territories—fighting a war sparked by dueling deities. When Peleus (PEE-lee-us) and Thetis (THEE-tiss) neglected to invite Eris (AYR-iss), the goddess of discord, to their wedding, she became enraged. To avenge the insult, she crashed their wedding reception and left behind a golden apple, inscribed "for the fairest." Immediately Hera (HAYR-uh), Athena (uh-THEE-nuh), and Aphrodite (aa-froh-DY-tee) all reached for the apple, and the three vain goddesses began to argue. To settle the dispute, Zeus declared that Paris, the Prince of Troy, would be the judge to decide who should get the apple.

In hopes of swaying him, all three goddesses promised Paris a gift. Hera promised him power, Athena promised him wealth (or in some versions, victory in battle), and Aphrodite promised him the love of the most beautiful woman in the world. Since Paris was considered to be the handsomest man in the known universe, the woman seemed a fitting prize, so Paris judged Aphrodite the winner. She, in turn, kept her promise and granted him the most beautiful woman, Helen. There was only one problem. Helen was already married—to Menelaus (meh-nuh-LAY-us), the powerful king of Sparta. Paris didn't care. Determined to have his prize, he sailed to Sparta.

Unaware of what Paris wanted, Menelaus welcomed the Trojan prince as a royal guest. When Menelaus left Sparta to attend a funeral, Paris abducted Helen. He also took a large sum of Menelaus' money. In some versions of the story, it is suggested that Helen left willingly with Paris. After all, it was Aphrodite, the goddess of love, who had promised her to Paris. In *Troy: Its Legend, History and Literature*, S.G.W. Benjamin notes: "Infatuated by the personal attractions of her foreign guest, Helen consented to fly her kingdom and family and return with him to Troy. . . . The love of the guilty pair . . . was undoubtedly genuine. . . . They both understood that they had been predestined for each other, and had the divine sanction for their love."[1]

Whether she left by force or by choice, once they returned to Troy, Paris and Helen were married. Menelaus was understandably outraged. His brother, the powerful Agamemnon (aa-guh-MEM-non) who ruled Mycenae (MY-seh-nay), called on the kings of the other Greek city-states to join him in defending Helen's honor. They also recruited the great Greek hero Achilles (uh-KIL-eez) after the seer Calchas (KAL-kus) told Agamemnon the Greeks would lose without his help. With their troops assembled, they set sail for Troy. Once there, Menelaus tried to prevent war by first asking King Priam (PRY-um) to return Helen and the money. Priam refused, and one of the most famous conflicts in recorded history began.

For over a decade the Greeks tried to invade Troy, but the city was surrounded by a thick, impenetrable wall. The Greeks refused to leave until Helen was returned, so the two armies were at a stand-off. It would take the ingenuity of another Greek hero named Odysseus (oh-DIH-see-us) to use cunning and deception to end the war and vanquish Troy. Knowing they would never be able to pierce its walls, Odysseus decided the only way to get inside the city was by trickery.

Among the Greeks, Odysseus was considered one of the most cunning. He was not impulsive and emotional the way Achilles could be; instead he was more methodical, using his intelligence to outwit opponents rather than always trying to outfight them. It was a trait he shared with Athena, the Greek goddess of wisdom, who was Odysseus' special protector.

For the citizens of Troy, the siege had become part of their daily lives. When they woke one day to discover that all the Greek soldiers had disbanded their camp and apparently set sail for Greece, they were first stunned, then joyous. Most surprising, though, was the gigantic wooden horse the Greeks had left outside the gates to the city. It was said to be a gift to the goddess Athena from the defeated Greeks. Grateful the war was over and deliriously happy to have beaten the powerful Greeks, the gates to the city were opened and the horse was pulled into the center of town.

Not everyone believed the horse was a peace offering. In Virgil's *Aeneid*, Laocoon (lay-OH-koh-on) warns: "I fear the Greeks, especially when they bear gifts,"[2] and he cast his spear into the horse's side. Priam's daughter Cassandra (kuh-SAN-druh) also warned her father that bringing the horse in would lead to the destruction of Troy. The god Apollo (uh-PAH-loh) had given Cassandra the ability to see the future, but when she spurned his romantic advances, he cursed her so that no one in Troy would believe her prophecies.

> Yet, mad with zeal, and blinded with our fate,
> We haul along the horse in solemn state;
> Then place the dire portent within the tow'r.
> Cassandra cried, and curs'd th' unhappy hour;
> Foretold our fate; but, by the god's decree,
> All heard, and none believ'd the prophecy.[3]

Meanwhile, two great serpents reared up out of the sea and swallowed Laocoon and his sons, which the Trojans believed was his punishment for spearing Athena's offering. Sinon, a Greek who pretended he was a deserter, told the Trojans the offering was real. Convinced the horse was safe, the rejoicing Trojans hauled the horse into the center of town and began celebrating. Cassandra, who knew better, went to pray at the altar of Athena.

That night, the people of Troy celebrated their victory by feasting on food and wine—just as Odysseus had planned. While the Trojans drank themselves into a stupor, inside the wooden horse, a group of Greek soldiers, led by Odysseus, sat silently and waited until the revelers passed out from either exhaustion or drunkenness. When the night grew silent, Sinon opened the trapdoor, and Odysseus jumped to the ground, followed by his men. There was a full moon overhead, so they could see everything around them. They immediately killed the sentries at the gates and then opened the doors, allowing in the rest of the Greek soldiers, who had silently sailed their ships back to shore.

Defenseless, the Trojans were slaughtered. Nearly every male in the city was killed, including children. The swords of the Greeks ran red with blood and the night echoed with screams of terror and death. Menelaus had vowed to kill Helen for her betrayal, but when he finally confronted her, he once again was so taken with her beauty, he spared her life and they left Troy together. She returned to Sparta as queen.

But not all the Greeks lived happily ever after. Achilles was killed by Paris on the battlefield. When Agamemnon returned home, he was murdered by his wife, Clytemnestra, for having sacrificed their daughter in order to get favorable winds for the voyage to Troy. And it took Odysseus ten years after the end of the war to get home.

The story of the Trojan War and Odysseus' long journey home are the subject of Homer's epic poems *The Iliad* and *The Odyssey*. The poems were more than just engrossing adventures. Listening to Homer recount the brave deeds of the combatants made ancient Greeks all around the Aegean see themselves in Homer's heroes and inspired them to carry on those ideals in their own city-states. A newfound sense of nationality and common culture resulted. For that, Homer would become revered throughout all of Greece—and Odysseus would become a hero for the ages.

Homer

Homer is credited with being the first ancient poet to write his verses down for posterity.

Homer was probably born sometime around 850 BCE. His mother, Critheis (KRIH-thee-is), named him Melesigenes (meh-leh-SIH-jeh-neez) because he was born near the Meles River in Smyrna, which was located in modern-day Turkey. Critheis later married a literature and music teacher named Phemius (FEE-mee-us), who adopted her son. The boy started attending Phemius' school, where he excelled in his studies. When Phemius died, he left the school to Melesigenes. Critheis died not long after, and Melesigenes supported himself by running the school and teaching.

One day Melesigenes met a man named Mentes (MEN-tees), and they became good friends. Mentes convinced Melesigenes to close the school and go see the world. They sailed to Ithaca, an island off the northwest coast of Greece, and the traditional home of Odysseus. Melesigenes' adventure was short-lived—he began having trouble with his eyesight. Before Mentes left to continue his travels, he arranged for Melesigenes to stay with another friend, Mentor, who entertained his guest with stories about the local hero Odysseus.

When Melesigenes returned to Smyrna, he studied poetry. Eventually he went blind. Unable to teach anymore, Melesigenes fell on hard times. Penniless, he traveled to Cyme, where he began reciting verses. It was there that he was given the name Homer, because that's what the locals called all blind men.

Most of the time, he would recite his poetry at the agora, or town meeting place. Like many other storytellers, or bards, Homer sang stories about the Trojan War and its heroes. The songs, which were the poems accompanied by music on a lyre, were so long it would take several evenings to tell the story. The people who listened to Homer never tired of hearing about the heroic deeds of their ancestors, and the poems instilled a kind of national pride that had never been part of the Ionian culture. Ironically, when the Romans conquered the Greeks, they too were inspired by Homer's tale and also came to revere Odysseus, whom they called Ulysses.

Sisyphus, painted by Titian around 1490. According to some versions of Odysseus'
life, the hero's real father was Sisyphus and not Laertes. Like Odysseus, Sisyphus was
known for his cunning, and he was a trickster. His endless punishment in the
Underworld of rolling a boulder uphill would keep the trickster out of trouble.

ODYSSEUS

CHAPTER 2
A Modest Childhood

Not much has been written about Odysseus' early years. According to the *Odyssey*, his mother was Anticleia (an-tih-KLY-uh), and his father was Laertes (LAY-er-teez), one of the Argonauts who had accompanied the hero Jason in retrieving the Golden Fleece. However, some later accounts say Odysseus' father was actually Sisyphus (SIH-suh-fus), the first king of Corinth. An unlikable man who enjoyed killing travelers passing through his territory, Sisyphus was famous for his cunning and conniving—like the time Zeus (ZOOS), the supreme god, found out Sisyphus had betrayed one of his secrets. He ordered Thanatos (Death) to take Sisyphus to the Underworld and chain him there as a punishment.

When they got there, Sisyphus suggested that Thanatos try on the chains to make sure they worked. When he did, Sisyphus locked them and escaped. With Thanatos chained to the wall, no mortals could die, and chaos followed. Finally, Ares (AIR-eez), the god of war, went to the Underworld and freed Thanatos. Sisyphus received an even worse punishment for his trickery. He was condemned to spend eternity rolling a huge boulder up a steep hill; and right before the boulder reached the top, it would roll back to the bottom. The term *Sisyphean task* refers to an endless task or one that's impossible to achieve.

Odysseus was born and raised in Ithaca. Not long after his birth, Anticleia's father, Autolycus (aw-TOL-uh-kus), came to visit. Odysseus' grandfather was a colorful character—and a notorious professional thief. Autolycus had the ability to change the color or shape of whatever he stole, a gift given to him by *his* father, the god Hermes. While visiting Anticleia and Laertes, their nurse Eurycleia (yuh-rih-KLY-yuh) handed Autolycus his grandson and told the crafty thief to name him. He replied:

> Daughter and son-in-law of mine,
> Give this child the name I now tell you.
> I come here as one who is odious, yes,
> Hateful to many for the pain I have caused
> All over the land. Let this child, therefore,
> Go by the name of Odysseus ["son of pain"].[1]

From an early age Odysseus excelled in archery and would go hunting with his dog Argos. When he was older, he once went to visit Autolycus, who lived near Mount Parnassus. He was greeted warmly by his grandmother Amphithea (am-FIH-thee-uh) and his uncles. Autolycus told his sons to prepare a meal, so they roasted a bull and feasted the rest of the day. Early the next morning, Odysseus went hunting with his uncles in the woods on the mountain.

> The dogs were out front,
> Tracking the scent, and behind the dogs
> Came Autolycus' sons and noble Odysseus,
> His brandished spear casting a long shadow.[2]

The woods were so thick with trees that very little sunlight filtered down through the leaves. In the murky light, they spotted a wild boar. Before Odysseus could throw his spear, the boar charged and gored his thigh. Despite his injury, Odysseus was able to spear and kill the animal. He stayed at his grandfather's house until the wound healed, then returned to Ithaca.

Odysseus matured into an average-looking young man who was said to be a bit bow-legged. According to Homer, Odysseus ruled the Cephallenians (seh-feh-LEE-nee-uns), who lived on the islands off the northwest coast of mainland Greece. He lived in a palace on Ithaca. Compared to many other Greek rulers, Odysseus was not particularly wealthy, and he ruled over a modest kingdom. He was

Odysseus' mother, Anticleia, was the granddaughter of the god Hermes. While Odysseus was away fighting the Trojan War, Anticleia died of grief, despondent over his extended absence.

known for his sharp intelligence and being an exceptional conversationalist. His quick mind and cleverness especially endeared him to Athena, the goddess of wisdom.

When the time came for Odysseus to settle down with a wife and start a family, he traveled to Sparta and briefly joined the long list of men competing for Helen's hand in marriage. However, his heart was not in it; Odysseus was more interested in Helen's cousin, Penelope. He was aware that Helen's father, King Tyndareus (tin-DAYR-ee-us), was worried that after he chose Helen's future husband, the rejected suitors might get angry and cause trouble, so he offered to make a deal with Tyndareus: If the king would help him win the hand of his niece Penelope, Odysseus would give Tyndareus a solution to his problems.

After the king agreed, Odysseus told him to make every one of Helen's suitors promise to defend and protect whoever was chosen as Helen's husband, should anyone threaten the marriage. This promise became known as the Oath of Tyndareus. All the suitors, including Odysseus, took the oath. Helen eventually married Menelaus. Because Tyndareus did not have any male children of his own who could ascend to his throne, he gave his Spartan kingdom to Menelaus to rule.

Odysseus watches his father, Laertes, in his vineyard. Laertes was king of the Cephallenians. His kingdom included Ithaca and some surrounding islands. In his youth, Laertes was an Argonaut and also hunted the Calydonian Boar. When he settled down, he raised livestock and taught the skill to Odysseus.

Having kept his end of the bargain, Odysseus went to win Penelope's hand. Her father, Icarius (ih-KAYR-ee-us) of Lacedaemon (lah-kuh-DAY-mon), an area near Sparta, decreed that he would offer his daughter to the first man who could beat him in a footrace. Odysseus succeeded and married Penelope. Upset at the thought of his daughter leaving Sparta, Icarius tried to make the newlyweds settle in Lacedaemon. Odysseus refused. When he and Penelope started to ride away in their chariot, Icarius ran after them, begging his daughter to stay.

Moved by her father's love, Odysseus told Penelope he would not force her to go and gave her the choice of either staying in Sparta or joining Odysseus in Ithaca. Penelope chose to leave with him. When the couple arrived in Ithaca, Odysseus made their marriage bed by hand out of a huge olive tree he cut down and carved. Then he built a house around the bed.

The young couple had a son, Telemachus (tuh-LEH-muh-kus), and were enjoying a happy life together. Then word came that Paris had seduced Helen and taken her back to Troy. Menelaus and his brother Agamemnon were calling on everyone who had taken the Oath of Tyndareus to help them get her back. It was especially important that Odysseus go because an oracle had prophesied that Troy could not be defeated without him. However, there was another

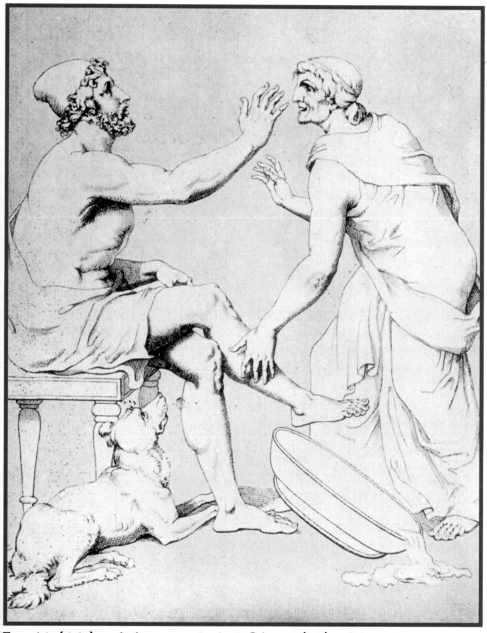

Eurycleia (right) worked as a nurse for both Odysseus (left) and, later, his son Telemachus. Entrusted to run the household, she was fiercely loyal. Years after Odysseus was gored by a boar, Eurycleia would recognize the scar on his leg.

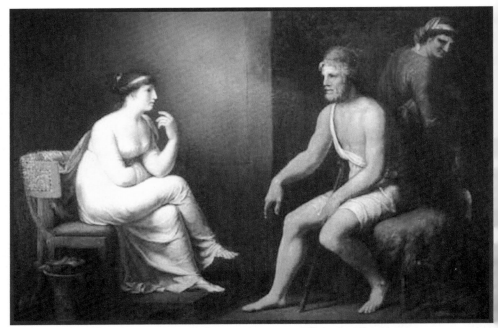

Odysseus and Penelope, painted by Johann Heinrich Wilhelm Tischbein in 1802. Penelope was Helen's first cousin and King Tyndareus' niece. She would remain faithful to her husband for twenty years while he was fighting and returning from the Trojan War.

prophesy—that if Odysseus went to Troy, he would not return home for twenty years, and in the interim, he would lose all his men and ships.

Odysseus tried to get out of going by pretending he had lost his mind. He plowed his field with an ox and a donkey and sowed salt instead of seeds. But one of Agamemnon's lieutenants, Palamedes (puh-LAA-muh-deez), knew that Odysseus was faking. To prove it, he put Telemachus, who was still an infant, in the path of the plow. Odysseus turned the plow aside to avoid hurting his son, thereby proving he wasn't insane. Having no choice but to keep the oath, Odysseus held a meeting with the leading men of Ithaca and instructed them to take care of his family and household. Then he gathered his soldiers and set sail for Troy.

Jason and the Argonauts

Jason bringing Pelias
the Golden Fleece

The story of Jason and the Argonauts and their quest for the Golden Fleece is one of the most popular in all of Greek mythology.

Jason was the son of Aeson (EE-son), the rightful king of Iolcus. But his uncle Pelias (PEE-lee-us) had stolen the throne from Aeson and imprisoned him. Pelias would have killed Jason, but Jason's mother pretended he had died at birth. She sent Jason to live with Cheiron (KY-ron) the Centaur, who had the upper body of a man and the lower body of a horse. Cheiron raised Jason, teaching him how to hunt and schooling him in the arts.

When Jason came of age, he set out to reclaim the throne his uncle had stolen. Pelias recognized Jason as his nephew, but he couldn't immediately kill the young man because some foreign kings were visiting. Instead, he challenged Jason to steal the Golden Fleece, which belonged to King Aeëtes (ee-EE-teez) of Colchis. According to an oracle's prophecy, Iolcus would never prosper until it possessed the precious fleece, which was guarded night and day by a dragon. Pelias swore before Zeus that he would give up the throne when Jason returned—for he was sure his nephew would be killed trying to take the fleece.

When the news of Jason's quest spread, dozens of Greek heroes, including Hercules and Perseus (PER-see-us), offered to accompany Jason. Their ship was *Argo,* and the men aboard were called the Argonauts. On their journey they experienced many adventures, and Jason was frequently helped by Hera, the queen of the gods. When they finally arrived in Colchis, Hera saw to it that Aeëtes' daughter Medea fell in love with Jason. She promised to help him steal the fleece if Jason promised to marry her. He agreed, and after capturing the fleece returned with Medea to Iolcus. They had two children together, then Jason left her for another woman. Medea took revenge on Jason by killing her children. That tragic story was immortalized by Greek playwright Euripides (yur-RIP-ih-deez) in the drama *Medea,* which was first performed in 431 BCE.

Thetis comes to take Achilles back from Cheiron, the boy's teacher. Cheiron was the kindes
the centaurs, creatures that had the legs and body of a horse and the head, chest, and arms of
man. A healer and teacher, Cheiron tutored many heroes, including Hercules and Jason.

ODYSSEUS

CHAPTER 3

The Wrath of Achilles

After securing the service of Odysseus, Agamemnon sent him on a mission to recruit the teenaged Achilles, who was the son of Peleus, the king of the Myrmidons (MEER-mih-dons), and the sea goddess (or nymph) Thetis. Calchas had prophesized that Troy could not be conquered without Achilles' help. However, since Achilles had not been one of Helen's suitors, he was not bound by the Oath of Tyndareus. Plus, his mother did not want him to go to war because a different oracle had told her that her son would either die young a great hero or live a long, but anonymous, life. There are two versions of how Thetis tried to protect Achilles.

In the first, Thetis anointed the baby Achilles with ambrosia, the food of the gods believed to give immortality, then placed him in a fire, which burned away the part of him that was mortal. Peleus discovered what she was doing and, horrified, stopped her. Irate, she left her family. Peleus then placed Achilles in the care of Cheiron, the centaur, who raised the young boy and educated him. In the second, later version, Thetis immersed him in the Styx, the river that formed the boundary between Earth and the Underworld. The water's magical powers made Achilles invulnerable—except for his heel where Thetis held him.

When Thetis learned that Odysseus was coming to recruit Achilles, she disguised him as a young woman. Odysseus figured out the ruse, and Achilles was faced with a choice: "My mother Thetis tells me that there are two ways in which I may meet my end. If I stay here and fight, I shall not return alive but my name will live forever: whereas if I go home my name will die, but it will be long ere death shall take me."[1]

The Discovery of Achilles among the Daughters of Lycomedes, painted in 1664 by Jan de Bray. The cunning Odysseus tricked Achilles (in white) into revealing his identity.

He chose glory. Achilles assembled a group of his father's soldiers, including his close friend Patroclus (PAH-truh-klus), and led the Myrmidons to Troy. Meanwhile, Odysseus made one last attempt to avoid what everyone knew would be a long, bloody, and costly conflict. He accompanied Menelaus and Palamedes to meet with King Priam. Odysseus made an impassioned plea that nearly persuaded the Trojans to return Helen. But in the end, she stayed with Paris in Troy, and the war was on.

When the Greeks landed on the shores of Troy, Odysseus was the first to disembark the ships. None of the other men would leave the ships because of a prophecy that said the first Greek to set foot on Trojan soil would die. Odysseus, using the cunning he was famous for, tossed his shield onto the sand and stepped on it. Protesilaus (proh-TEH-sih-lous) followed him and later became the first Greek to die.

On the battlefield, Achilles earned the reputation of being a fierce, unbeatable warrior. Not only was he protected by the water from the Styx, his mother had also presented him with special armor from the god Hephaestus (heh-FES-tus). When he wasn't fighting outside the walls of Troy, Achilles took his army through the Trojan territory and captured over twenty towns. Upon conquering Lyrnessos, he took a woman named Briseis

Achilles and Thetis by Benjamin West. Thetis brings Achilles armor made by Hephaestus, god of the forge.

(brih-SAY-iss) as a war-prize after killing her husband. She became his mistress, and over time, they fell in love. Briseis would become a source of deep conflict between Achilles and Agamemnon.

Agamemnon was considered the overall leader of the Greek forces. After one of Apollo's oracles forced him to give up his war-prize, a woman named Chryseis (krih-SAY-iss), Agamemnon took Briseis to fill her place. Achilles became enraged and refused to fight any more against Troy. Achilles' anger toward Agamemnon and the Greeks' desperation to get him to return is where the story of *The Iliad* begins. Achilles is furious that Agamemnon did to him what Paris had done to Menelaus—which is why the Greeks were fighting the Trojans in the first place. He rails:

"Why has he gathered and led here his host . . . ? Was it not for Helen's sake? Do they then alone of mortal men love their wives . . . ? No, for he who is a true man loves his own and cherishes her, as I too loved Briseis with all my heart."[2]

Without his skill and leadership, the Greeks begin to lose to the Trojans, and they are desperate to get him back. Agamemnon sends Odysseus and other ambassadors to bargain with Achilles. Odysseus cunningly couches his message as a "reminder" of what the warrior's father must have told him before he left for Troy—to

"hold in check
that proud, fiery spirit of yours inside your chest!
Friendship is much better. Vicious quarrels are deadly—
put an end to them at once. . . ."
That was your aged father's parting advice.
It must have slipped your mind.
        But now at last,
stop Achilles—let your heart-devouring anger go![3]

On behalf of Agamemnon, Odysseus then offered Achilles an assortment of gifts, including the return of Briseis, who was still untouched by Agamemnon. But Achilles did not trust Odysseus—the two had a rivalry, with Achilles placing more faith in his physical strength than in Odysseus' famed cunning.

Even though Briseis wanted Achilles to return to battle and come retrieve her, he continued his boycott. Instead, he sent a group of Myrmidon soldiers led by Patroclus, who was wearing Achilles' armor. During the next day's fighting, the Trojan prince Hector killed Patroclus and took the treasured armor.

When Achilles learned of his friend's death, he was overcome with grief and directed his rage at Hector. Thetis obtained new armor for her son from Hephaestus, and Achilles returned to the battlefield. He killed Hector, then desecrated the body by dragging it behind his

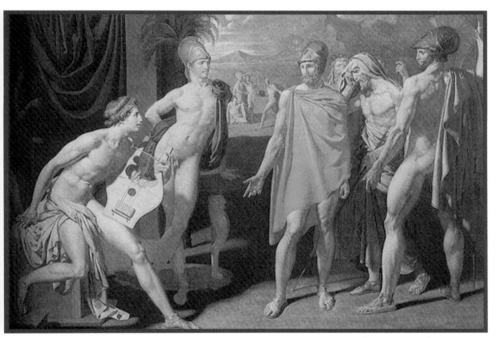

The Ambassadors of Agamemnon in the Tent of Achilles, painted in 1801 by Jean-August-Dominique Ingres. In Book 9 of *The Iliad,* Achilles (left) is still angry with Agamemnon for stealing Briseis. Instead of fighting, he lounges in his tent, playing the lyre for Patroclus (who is wearing Achilles' helmet). Odysseus (center) must convince Achilles to return to the battle.

chariot. He also prevented Hector from receiving any funeral rites. It wasn't until King Priam snuck into the Greek camp to beg for his son's body that Achilles relented.

Achilles fought tirelessly, killing scores of Trojans and ensuring his name would be known forever. His glory, in turn, would ensure that his days were numbered. The end came when Paris, with the help of Apollo, shot an arrow in Achilles' unprotected heel. The injury killed Achilles.

After Achilles' death, it was decided that his armor would be given to the bravest Greek. Only two competed for the prize: Odysseus and Ajax. Each gave a speech explaining why he should get the armor. As Ovid tells the story in *Metamorphoses,* Odysseus began his speech this way:

> "Since unjust fate has denied [Achilles] both to me and you, (and here he wiped his eyes dry with his hands, as though then shedding tears,) who could succeed the great Achilles better than the one through whom the great Achilles joined the Greeks? Let Ajax win no votes because he seems to be as stupid as the truth declares. Let not my talents, which were always used for service of the Greeks, increase my harm: and let this eloquence of mine (if such we call it) which is pleading now for me, as it has pleaded many times for you, awake no envy."[4]

He then detailed how he had not been fooled by Achilles' disguise in Lycomedes' palace, and how he convinced Achilles to come to Troy, despite the prophecy that by fighting he would die young; how he spoke to the hero when the angry Achilles refused to fight; and many other brave and crafty deeds, including how he carried the dead Achilles, in all his armor, off the battlefield. (He says this, though some say Ajax carried his corpse.)

Odysseus won the contest. Ajax was so despondent over losing that he committed suicide.

The Greeks had a bigger problem—defeating the Trojans without Achilles. Odysseus used his cunning—and, some stories say, the help of Athena—to come up with the idea of the wooden horse, which led to the destruction of Troy and the end of the ten-year conflict.

The Greeks celebrated their victory by committing many atrocities, such as raping Cassandra, who was a priestess of Apollo. The angry god sent a storm that destroyed most of the Greek fleet as they returned home. Odysseus was the only one who had called for the rapist to be executed, so Apollo spared him and his men. But Odysseus would run afoul of another god, and it would be another ten long years before he would see home.

Ancient Greek Weapons

Ancient Greece was a violent place, with war practically a way of life, both among individual Greek city-states and among Greeks and other European people. Developing a strong army and efficient weaponry was vitally important. Unlike modern warfare, which is conducted at great distances with guns and bombs, fighting in ancient Greece was much more intimate.

Greek hoplite

The most important soldiers were called hoplites, foot soldiers who engaged in most of the fighting. They marched into battle during broad daylight, facing their enemy directly. They lived or died on their hand-to-hand combat skills and bravery. They usually wore heavy armor, which weighed approximately sixty-five pounds and included helmets, breastplates and back plates, and shin guards called greaves. They carried a large shield, which was used as a defensive weapon. Going into battle, hoplites marched in lines with their shields overlapping to form a protective metal wall.

Although they carried a short sword and dagger at their side, their preferred weapon was a spear. Greek spears were six to eight feet long, and the tip was sharpened iron. The spears frequently broke. When that happened, the handle could be used as a club.

Hoplites had to pay for their own armor, so many of the soldiers were from more prosperous middle-class families. Those from poor families became archers and wore no armor. Only the wealthy could afford horses, so the cavalrymen were aristocrats. They carried two throwing spears and a sword.

Eventually, other weaponry was developed, such as the ballista, which was modeled after a crossbow and looked somewhat like a giant slingshot. It shot either dartlike projectiles or large stones. This weapon was used mostly during sieges—such as at Troy when the Greeks were trying to penetrate the city's walls—and not so much on an active battlefield.

A ballista

Odysseus pours wine for Polyphemus the Cyclops. Odysseus was cunning enough to save most of his men from Polyphemus, but his actions also angered the god Poseidon. The Greeks' unfortunate landing on the Island of the Cyclopes would doom their return from Troy.

ODYSSEUS

CHAPTER 4

Odyssey

After the destruction of Troy, Odysseus and his men set sail for the journey home in twelve ships. The seas were calm, leading Odysseus to believe they were in the gods' good graces. His second in command, Eurylochus (yuh-RIH-luh-kus), convinced Odysseus to go ashore to loot the city of Ismara for supplies. The city and nearby area was the home of the Cicones (see-KOH-neez, or kih-KOH-neez), who had fought with Troy against the Greeks. Odysseus and his men attacked with a vengeance. The Ciconian men who didn't escape into the mountains were killed; the women were raped. The only one spared was Maron, a priest of Apollo. In return, Maron gave Odysseus a dozen jars of wine.

After pillaging the city, Odysseus told his men to get back aboard the ship. They refused, and instead camped out on the beach, where they had dinner, got drunk, and went to sleep. The next morning the residents of Ismara returned with reinforcements. As Odysseus relates in *The Odyssey*:

"Some of the town's survivors got away inland
And called their kinsmen. There were more of them,
And they were braver, too, men who knew how to fight
From chariots and on foot. They came on as thick
As leaves and flowers in spring, attacking . . .
We lost six fighting men from each of our ships.
The rest of us cheated destiny and death."[1]

His next stop was the island of the Lotus Eaters. He sent some men ashore to look for food. When they ate the lotus flower, they fell under its powerful properties. Like a drug, they became addicted, not caring about anything but finding more flowers to eat. Odysseus finally had to go ashore and forcibly drag the men back to the ship. To prevent them from jumping overboard and swimming back to the island, Odysseus had them tied to benches.

When Odysseus came to the Island of the Cyclopes, he took twelve men ashore to look for food. They came across a large cave, which was the home of the giant Cyclops Polyphemus (pah-lih-FEE-mus), a son of Poseidon. When the Cyclops, who only had one eye in the middle of his forehead, came home and discovered Odysseus and his men, he blocked the entrance with a large boulder. He then ate two of the men.

To save himself and the others, Odysseus came up with an ingenious plan. First, he offered some wine to Polyphemus, who asked his name. Odysseus answered, "Noman." After the Cyclops passed out, Odysseus directed his men to sharpen the giant's club to a point. They then stabbed it into the Cyclops' eye, blinding him. Polyphemus called out to his fellow Cyclopes for help, saying Noman had hurt him. Assuming he was drunk or under a spell from a god, the other Cyclopes ignored him.

In the morning, Odysseus and his men tied themselves beneath Polyphemus' sheep. Before he let his sheep out to graze, he felt their coats to make sure his prisoners weren't riding out on them. But he didn't check beneath, where the Greeks were clutching the wool. The Greeks hurried back to their ships and set sail.

Basking in his successful escape, Odysseus yelled to Polyphemus: "Noman didn't hurt you, Odysseus did!" This display of ego would cost Odysseus dearly. Poseidon was already annoyed at Odysseus for not offering him a sacrifice after protecting the Greeks while they were inside the wooden horse. When Polyphemus asked his father for revenge, the god complied. He sent foul weather to hinder Odysseus from getting home.

Odysseus found a friendlier reception on the island of Aeolia (ee-OH-lee-uh), home to Aeolus (ee-OH-lus), god of the winds. Aeolus entertained Odysseus and his crew for a month, and Odysseus regaled him with stories. When the crew finally prepared to go, Aeolus gave Odysseus a bag containing stormy winds; with those contained, Odysseus could sail safely home.

Odysseus protected the bag around the clock. Some of his crew members, who did not know the bag's contents, suspected Odysseus was hoarding treasure. They were almost home when Odysseus fell asleep. His crewmen opened the bag, allowing the stormy winds to escape, and the fleet was pushed all the way back to Aeolia. Aware that Odysseus was being punished by one of the gods, Aeolus refused to help the Greeks again.

Forced to begin the journey home all over, Odysseus' fleet came to Telepylos (teh-leh-PY-lohs), the home of a race of giant cannibals called the Laestrygonians (ly-strih-GOH-nee-uns). Odysseus anchored his ship outside the island's natural harbor, which was protected by steep cliffs and had a single, narrow entrance. The other eleven ships moored side by side in the harbor, where the water was perfectly still. Odysseus sent three men to scout out the island. One of the men was eaten by a cannibal. The other two ran back to the ship, but thousands of cannibals appeared along the cliffs ringing the harbor. They threw rocks at the ships and speared the Greeks. All the men aboard the eleven ships were killed. Only Odysseus' ship escaped.

They sailed to Aeaea (ee-EE-uh), the island where sorceress Circe (SIR-see, or KIR-kee) lived. Odysseus again sent a scouting party ashore. Circe invited the men to a feast, then turned them into pigs. One escaped and returned to the ship. Before Odysseus went to save his crewmen, the god Hermes gave him a special herb that made him invulnerable to Circe's magic.

Unable to control him, Circe fell in love with Odysseus. After she turned his men back into humans, Odysseus and Circe began an affair that lasted a year and resulted in the birth of a son named Telegonus (teh-LEH-goh-nus). Eventually, his crew became impatient and demanded they resume their journey home.

After visiting the Underworld to ask the prophet Teiresias (ty-REE-see-us) how to get back to Ithaca, Odysseus continued on his journey, which took him past the Island of the Sirens. Each Siren had the head of a woman but the body of a bird. Sailors were unable to resist their song, which the Sirens used to lure them to their deaths. Circe had warned Odysseus about the Sirens, so he had himself tied to the mast of his ship and ordered his men to fill their ears with beeswax. They made it through without loosing a man.

Odysseus then faced a choice of which route to take home. One way would take him through the wandering rocks, which crushed ships as they tried to pass through them. Odysseus took the other route, which was also extremely dangerous. He had to sail through a strait that on one side had a whirlpool called Charybdis (kuh-RIB-diss), which was so powerful it would sink the ship. On the other side was a monster called Scylla (SIH-luh). Athena warned him:

Ulysses and the Sirens, by John William Waterhouse, painted in 1891. The Sirens were winged creatures that lured sailors to their deaths. Today, the term *siren song* refers to an appeal that is hard to resist but that, if heeded, will lead to an unwanted result.

"She barks and yelps
Like a young puppy, but she is a monster,
An evil monster that not even a god
Would be glad to see. She has—listen to this—
Twelve gangly legs and six very long necks,
And on each neck is perched a bloodcurdling head,
Each with three rows of close-set teeth."[2]

If Odysseus passed too close to Charybdis, no one would live. If he passed too close to Scylla, six of his men would die, but the rest of his crew would survive. As the ship steered clear of Charybdis, Scylla plucked six men out of the ship and ate them alive. Although the rest of the crew survived, they were upset and resentful at having seen their comrades' deaths. As a result, when they came to the Island of Helios, god of the sun, they ignored Odysseus' warning not to eat the god's cattle. Helios was so upset by their theft, he threatened to leave the world in darkness. To punish the ship's crew, Zeus struck the ship with a lightning bolt, killing everyone but Odysseus.

Odysseus in Front of Scylla and Charybdis, painted by Johann Heinrich Füssili around 1796. The phrase *between Scylla and Charybdis* has come to mean being between two dangers and finding that moving away from one will cause you to be in danger of the other.

He drifted in the sea until he washed up on Ogygia (oh-JID-jyuh), home of the nymph Calypso (kuh-LIP-soh). She would not let Odysseus leave and promised him immortality. He stayed with her for

Odysseus and Nausicaa, painted by Christoph Amberger in 1619. After Poseidon sent a storm to destroy Odysseus' raft, the hero washed up on the island home of the Phaeacians. King Alcinous' daughter, Nausicaa, took him to the palace, which was protected by gold and silver dogs forged by Hephaestus.

seven years, until Hermes intervened and convinced Calypso to let Odysseus go. He built a simple raft and set sail for home.

Meanwhile, Poseidon was still angry at Odysseus and sent a storm. The man washed ashore on an island inhabited by the Phaeacians (fee-AY-shuns) and was found by Nausicaa (NAW-sih-kah), daughter of King Alcinous. They welcomed Odysseus, and during a feast, he told them who he was and about his ten-year odyssey. Known for giving strangers safe passage home, they sailed him to Ithaca in one of their fast ships.

Finally, after twenty years away, Odysseus was home. But his journey was not quite over.

The Discovery of Troy

Heinrich Schliemann

After the Greeks vanquished Troy, they burned the city to the ground. The destruction was so complete that modern scholars weren't sure whether Troy had ever really existed or if Homer had made it up. We now know Troy was a real city, thanks to Frank Calvert and Heinrich Schliemann.

Schliemann first became obsessed with discovering Troy as a young boy after listening to his father tell him stories about the beautiful city known for its prosperity and the impenetrable wall that encircled it. In 1868, when he was forty-six years old and financially secure, Schliemann was finally able to pursue his childhood dream. The biggest question was, where would Troy have been located? The few scientists and scholars who believed Troy had been a real place thought it would have most likely been in Turkey.

While traveling through Turkey, Schliemann visited a hill called Hisarlik, where he met a British archaeologist named Frank Calvert, who had spent fifteen years excavating the area. Calvert was so sure he had found the true location of Troy, he bought part of the land from the Turkish government. Calvert confided in Schliemann, explaining why he believed Troy lay buried beneath Hisarlik. His evidence included artifacts and passages from Homer's *Iliad*.

It took the inexperienced Schliemann two years of preparation before he was ready to dig. He returned to Hisarlik and began excavating, employing members of Calvert's crew. Over the next three years, Schliemann found evidence that several cities had been built on the site over the millennia. Near the bottom of the excavation were the ruins of an ancient city with massive walls, well-built houses, and hidden treasures of gold and silver. Schliemann was convinced he had found Troy.

Since then, over one hundred excavations have been made at the site and ten different settlements have been identified. Most scholars believe the seventh city was the legendary city of Troy. Their evidence includes unburied skeletal remains that indicate some type of massacre and clues that the city was destroyed by a huge fire.

Map of Antiquity

Corsica
Hades
Adriatic Sea
Cleones
Calypso
Mt Olympus
Aegean Sea
Sardinia
Tyrrhenian Sea
Troy
Lotus Eaters
Ionian Sea
Aeolias Island
Ithaca
Sicily
Crete
Thrinacian Island
Numidia
Mediterranean Sea

Troy was approximately 400 miles from Ithaca, but because Poseidon intervened, Odysseus' journey home took ten years. Although scholars are not certain of the present-day location of all the mythical lands Odysseus visited, they believe his route covered numerous islands and deadly sea passages in the Mediterranean.

ODYSSEUS

CHAPTER 5

Returning Home

During the absence of Odysseus, his son, Telemachus, had grown into an able young man. His wife, Penelope, had remained faithful and continued to wait for his return. But many in Ithaca assumed Odysseus was dead. Penelope was being pressured by a group of suitors to remarry. These included local men as well as powerful foreigners who wanted to take over the kingdom. Even though she resisted, the suitors converged on the palace, hoping to force her into marriage. While there, they helped themselves to food and wine, abusing the palace's hospitality. Telemachus was infuriated by the suitors' actions and called a meeting of all Ithaca men. He asked them to supply him with a ship so that he could go find out what had happened to Odysseus, who he also assumed was dead. They agreed, and that night he sailed away with a volunteer crew of twenty.

His first stop was Pylos, where King Nestor told him what he knew about the Greeks' return from Troy, including Agamemnon's murder at the hands of his wife. Nestor suggested Telemachus travel to Sparta to speak to Menelaus. He loaned the young prince a chariot and sent one of his sons to accompany him.

Menelaus greeted Telemachus warmly, with Helen commenting on how much he looked like Odysseus. Menelaus recounted how on the way home from Troy, a storm had pushed him to Egypt, where he was stranded for seven years. While there, he encountered a god and asked what had become of his Greek comrades. The god revealed that Odysseus was still alive but marooned on an island with no way home. Telemachus was relieved to know his father was alive, but the news didn't do much to solve the problem of the suitors, who were now plotting to kill Telemachus.

When Odysseus finally reached Ithaca, he was met by the goddess Athena. As they sat together under an olive tree, she explained what was happening with Penelope and the suitors, and they spoke of how to rid his house of them:

> "Resourceful Odysseus,
> consider how you can lay your hands on these shameless
>   suitors,
> who for three years now have been as lords in your palace,
> and courting your godlike wife, and offering gifts to win her."[1]

Athena disguised Odysseus as an old beggar, even "wither[ing] the handsome flesh that is on your flexible limbs,"[2] so that he could move around Ithaca and gather information about the suitors without being recognized. He went to one of his longtime servants, an old pig farmer named Eumaeus (yoo-MAY-us). Believing Odysseus was the old beggar he appeared to be, Eumaeus invited him in and cooked him dinner. Odysseus was touched by the man's gracious hospitality—and with his sorrow over Odysseus' failure to return.

When Telemachus returned from his trip, Athena directed him to the pig farm. Eumaeus was dispatched to go tell Penelope her son had returned safely. While he was gone, Athena transformed Odysseus back to his true self so that he could reveal his identity to Telemachus. Odysseus made his son promise not to tell anyone, even Penelope, about his return, and assured Telemachus he would deal with the suitors when the right time came.

Once again disguised as a beggar, Odysseus traveled to the city, accompanied by Eumaeus. As they entered the palace, Odysseus spotted his old hunting dog, Argos, lying in the dirt. The dog recognized him in return and struggled to his feet to meet his master, bringing tears to Odysseus' eyes.

Odysseus used his disguise to identify the suitors and to also see who among his staff had remained loyal to him and who had given

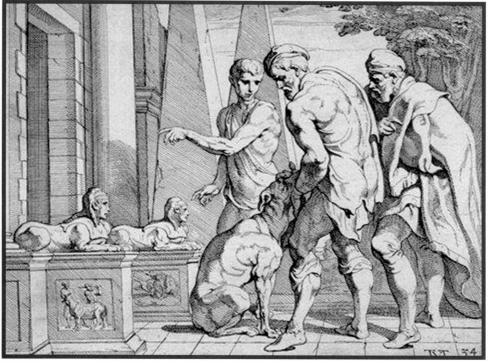

Telemachus and Eumaeus walk to the palace with Odysseus, who is disguised as a beggar. Odysseus' old hunting dog, Argos, recognizes his master.

their allegiance to the suitors. In addition to Eumaeus, only Philoetius (fih-loh-EE-shus), the cowherd, remained loyal. When Penelope entered the hall where the suitors were, Odysseus introduced himself to her as an acquaintance of her husband. She offered the beggar hospitality, completely unaware it was her husband standing before her. The only person who recognized him was his old nurse, Eurycleia, who saw the scar the boar had left on his thigh. Penelope was distraught because Odysseus had instructed her to take another husband after their son reached manhood if he did not return. She reluctantly accepted that the time had come to abide by her long lost husband's wishes.

She brought out Odysseus' bow and a quiver of arrows and announced that whoever among the suitors could shoot most accurately would win her hand in marriage:

> "Hear me now, you haughty suitors, who have been using
> this house for your incessant eating and drinking . . .
>   here is a prize set out before you;
> for I shall bring you the great bow of godlike Odysseus.
> And the one who takes the bow in his hands, strings it
>   with the greatest
> ease, and sends an arrow clean through all the twelve axes,
> shall be the one I go away with, forsaking this house
> where I was a bride, a lovely place and full of good living."[3]

One after another, the suitors were unable to draw back a single arrow. Then Odysseus stepped forward and asked for his turn. The suitors objected, ridiculing him, but Penelope agreed. Before Odysseus could shoot, Telemachus sent his mother and her chambermaids to their room, not wanting them to see the carnage he knew was about to happen. Odysseus strung the bow and shot true, then began shooting the suitors. Telemachus retrieved his father's armor and, alongside the faithful servants Eumaeus and Philoetius, helped Odysseus slaughter the suitors, killing them all.

After the bodies were removed and the palace cleansed, Odysseus went to Penelope. At first, she didn't believe he was really her husband. Since she hadn't seen him for twenty years, she wasn't really sure what he would look like, and was worried an imposter might try to fool her. It was only after Odysseus reminded her how he had built their bedroom around a great olive tree that she knew he was really her husband.

Their joyous reunion was tempered by the knowledge that the relatives of the men he had killed would want revenge. While

Penelope's suitors use tables from the royal hall to try to protect themselves from Odysseus' arrows. They are doomed, however, as Odysseus blocks their escape.

Odysseus went to visit his father Laertes, the families of the suitors gathered, intent on storming the palace and killing Odysseus. But an old warrior named Halitherses (hal-ih-THER-seez) stood and spoke:

> "Now hear what I have to say, men of Ithaca.
> You have only yourselves to blame, my friends,
> For what has happened. You would not obey me
> Nor Mentor, shepherd of the people, when we told you
> To make your sons stop their foolishness.
> It was what your sons did that was truly monstrous,
> Wasting the wealth and dishonoring the wife
> Of a great man, who they said would never return.
> Now listen to me and keep your peace. Some of you
> Are asking for trouble—and you just might find it."[4]

Half of the crowd listened and dispersed. The other half took up arms and went to fight Odysseus. Another battle ensued, but Odysseus, Telemachus, and Laertes were unbeatable. They would have slaughtered them all, but Athena stopped the battle, sending the survivors running home. Odysseus wanted to follow and kill them, but Zeus ordered him to put down his weapons and end his revenge. He did and, with his wandering over, lived a long and happy life.

There are two stories about his final days. In *The Odyssey*, Teiresias told Odysseus that he would die a peaceful death as an old man. But in another version, Odysseus was accidentally killed by Telegonus, his son with Circe. Wanting to prove himself on the battlefield, Telegonus and his men attacked Ithaca, not knowing it was the homeland of his father. At the time, Odysseus was in northern Greece, but he returned to defend Ithaca from the invaders. During the battle, Telegonus killed Odysseus with a spear point made of a stingray spine. Only after Odysseus died did Telegonus discover he'd killed his father. Distraught, he, Penelope, and Telemachus took the body of Odysseus back to Circe, who made Odysseus and his family immortal so that they could live together for eternity.

Unlike most other Greek heroes, who had a god or goddess as one parent, Odysseus was a fully mortal human, so Greeks felt a special kinship with him. He was truly of the people, so they could relate to his adventures and challenges. While Greeks admired physical prowess and respected courage and determination, they revered cunning and intelligence above all. Greeks saw all those qualities in Odysseus and, by extension, in themselves. He embodied the pride and spirit of the culture and was a hero all people could aspire to emulate, from ancient times to modern day.

Head of Odysseus

The Return Date

For centuries, scholars believed the events in *The Iliad* and *The Odyssey* were myths. It wasn't until amateur archaeologist Heinrich Schliemann located the site of Troy in the 1870s that the Trojan War became widely accepted as a historical event. Even so, *The Odyssey*'s hero, Odysseus, was still considered to be fictional. However, researchers now believe they have uncovered proof that Homer was recounting at least some factual events in his story.

Their claim is based on astronomical evidence gleaned from *The Odyssey*. At the end of Book 20, a seer named Theoclymenus (thee-uh-KLY-muh-nus) foresees the deaths of Penelope's suitors, and says: "The Sun has been obliterated from the sky, and an unlucky darkness invades the world."[5] Some historians felt his comment was allegorical, but others suggested his vision was prompted by a solar eclipse darkening the skies above Ithaca.

In the 1920s, astronomers Carl Schoch and Paul Neugebauer calculated that a solar eclipse had indeed occurred over the Ionian Islands on April 16, 1178 BCE, around noon—a little more than a decade after the destruction of Troy, which is generally believed to have occurred around 1190 BCE.

Critics claimed that nobody could be sure Homer was really referring to an eclipse. So in 2008, two scientists at Rockefeller University in New York decided to use other astronomical evidence in *The Odyssey*. Marcelo Magnasco and Constantino Baikouzis found references to constellations, Venus, Mercury, and a new moon the night before Theoclymenus' prophecy. (Solar eclipses happen only during a new moon phase.) Then they computed possible dates around the time of Troy's fall that matched all the criteria and came up with one: April 16, 1178 BCE—the same date as the eclipse.

"How could Homer have known about this eclipse, about planetary positions that happened some 100 years before him?" asked Magnasco. "If this is all true, it would change the timetable of what we think they knew about astronomy then."[6]

In 2005, amateur British archaeologist Robert Bittlestone announced that he had found the location of ancient Ithaca—the peninsula of Paliki on the Ionian island of Cephallonia. He believes that in ancient times Paliki was a separate island before earthquakes and landslides obliterated a narrow waterway separating it from Cephallonia. His theory fits with Homer's descriptions of Odysseus' homeland, but critics say more geological research needs to be done before accepting his theory.

NOTE: Although there are no recorded dates referring to the life of Odysseus, the following represents the order in which events are said to have occurred.

- Odysseus is born to Anticleia and King Laertes.

- He visits his grandfather Autolycus near Mount Parnassus, and is gored by a wild boar while hunting.

- As one of Helen's early suitors, he decides he'd rather marry her sister, Penelope, and makes a deal with Tyndareus to marry her and protect Helen; he devises the Oath of Tyndareus.

- Penelope and Odysseus' son, Telemachus, is born.

- Odysseus is drafted to fight the Trojans after Paris abducts Helen.

- With the help of Athena, Odysseus devises the plan for the Trojan Horse. After the Greek victory, he sails for home.

- He angers Poseidon after he blinds his Cyclops son, Polyphemus.

- Odysseus' ship is the only one to survive an attack by the cannibalistic Laestrygonians.

- He spends a year with Circe, with whom he has a son, Telegonus.

- He visits the Underworld to seek guidance for getting back to Ithaca.

- He is tormented by the call of the Sirens.

- Zeus destroys his ship after the crew eats Helios' cattle. Only Odysseus survives.

- He spends seven years with Calypso, until the gods order her to release him.

- He is returned to Ithaca by the Phaeacians.

- Athena tells him of the suitors pursuing Penelope. He dresses as a beggar to spy on the suitors and see which servants have remained loyal, but he reveals himself to Telemachus.

- He kills the suitors and reveals his true identity to Penelope.

- He vanquishes the suitors' relatives, who have come for revenge.

- He dies an old man. According to some versions, he, Penelope, and Telemachus are made immortal by Circe.

Chapter 1. Beware of Greeks Bearing Gifts

1. S.G.W. Benjamin, *Troy: Its Legend, History and Literature* (New York: Charles Scribner's Sons, 1880), pp. 16–17.

2. Virgil, *Aeneid,* Book II, line 49, as translated by Jennifer March in *Cassell's Dictionary of Classical Mythology* (London, Cassell & Co., 2001), p. 451.

3. Virgil, *Aeneid,* translated by John Dryden, Book II, http://classics.mit.edu/Virgil/aeneid.mb.txt

Chapter 2. A Modest Childhood

1. Homer. *Odyssey*, translated by Stanley Lombardo (Indianapolis: Hackett Publishing, 2000), Book 19, lines 406–409, p. 302.

2. Ibid., lines 435–438, p. 303.

Chapter 3. The Wrath of Achilles

1. Homer, *Iliad,* translated by Samuel Butler, Book 9, lines 497–505. http://classics.mit.edu/Homer/iliad.9.ix.html

2. Ibid., lines 410–416.

3. Homer, *The Iliad,* translated by Robert Fagles (New York: Penguin Books, 1990), Book 9, lines 309–317.

4. Ovid, *Metamorphoses,* translated by Brookes More, Book XIII, lines 130–139, http://www.theoi.com/Text/OvidMetamorphoses13.html#1

Chapter 4. Odyssey

1. Homer, *Odyssey,* translated by Stanley Lombardo (Indianapolis: Hackett Publishing, 2000), Book 9, lines 50–54 and 62–63, p. 126.

2. *The Essential Homer: Selections from the* Iliad *and the* Odyssey, translated by Stanley Lombardo (Indianapolis: Hackett Publishing), Book 12, lines 88–94, p. 180.

Chapter 5. Returning Home

1. Homer, *Odyssey of Homer,* translated by Richmond Lattimore (New York: HarperPerennial, 1991), Book 13, lines 375–378, p. 206.

2. Ibid., lines 398–399, p. 208.

3. Ibid., Book 21, lines 68–78, p. 311.

4. The Internet Classic Archive: *The Odyssey* by Homer, Book 24, lines 454–462. http://classics.mit.edu/Homer/odyssey.24.xxiv.html

5. The Internet Classics Archive, *The Odyssey*, Book 20, lines 356–357. http://classics.mit.edu/Homer/odyssey.20.xx.html

6. Charles Q. Choi, "Odysseus' Return from Trojan War Dated," *Live Science*, June 23, 2008, http://www.msnbc.msn.com/id/25337041/

FURTHER READING

Books

Connolly, Peter. *Ancient Greece of Odysseus*. New York: Oxford University Press, 1999.

Homer. *The Odyssey of Homer*. Adapted by Barbara Leonie Picard. New York: Oxford University Press, 2001.

Sutcliffe, Rosemary, and Alan Lee. *The Wanderings of Odysseus: The Story of the Odyssey*. London: Frances Lincoln, 2005.

Tracy, Kathleen. *The Life and Times of Homer*. Hockessin, Delaware: Mitchell Lane Publishers, 2005.

Works Consulted

Benjamin, S.G.W. *Troy: Its Legend, History and Literature*. New York: Charles Scribner's Sons, 1880.

Choi, Charles Q. "Odysseus' Return from Trojan War Dated: Time Pinpointed to the Day Based on References in Epic Poem." MSNBC: *LiveScience,* June 23, 2008. http://www.msnbc.msn.com/id/25337041/

"Has 'Odyssey' Hero's Land Been Found? Amateur Archaeologist Identifies Site of Ancient Ithaca." AP, MSNBC, September 30, 2005. http://www.msnbc.msn.com/id/9543382/

Homer. *The Iliad*. Translated by Robert Fagles. New York: Penguin Books, 1990.

Homer. *The Odyssey*. Translated by Samuel Butler. http://classics.mit.edu/Homer/odyssey.html

Homer. *The Odyssey*. Translated by Richmond Lattimore. New York: HarperPerennial, 1991.

Homer. *The Odyssey*. Translated by Stanley Lombardo. Indianapolis: Hackett Publishing, 2000.

March, Jenny. *Cassell's Dictionary of Classical Mythology*. London: Cassell & Co., 2001.

Ovid. *Heroides*. Translated by James M. Hunter. http://members.terracom.net/~hunter/heroides/heroides.htm

Ovid. *Metamorphoses*. Translated by Brookes More. http://www.theoi.com/Text/OvidMetamorphoses1.html

Quintus Smyrnaeus. *The Fall of Troy*. Translated by A. S. Way. http://www.theoi.com/Text/QuintusSmyrnaeus.html

Virgil. *Aeneid*. Translated by John Dryden. http://classics.mit.edu/Virgil/aeneid.mb.txt

On the Internet

Encyclopedia Mythica: "Odysseus," by James Hunter http://www.pantheon.org/articles/o/odysseus.html

Greek Mythology: Odysseus
    http://www.mythweb.com/odyssey/
Odysseus Unbound: The Search for Homer's Ithaca
    http://www.odysseus-unbound.org/

GLOSSARY

abducted (ub-DUK-ted)—Kidnapped.

ambrosia (am-BROH-jyuh)—The food of the gods.

banished (BAA-nisht)—Sent away permanently.

besieged (bee-SEEJD)—Surrounded by an enemy.

centaurs (SEN-tars)—Mythical creatures that were half human (top) and half horse (bottom).

city-state (SIH-tee STAYT)—A self-governing city that also rules the surrounding territory.

cunning (KUH-ning)—Cleverness.

cyclops (SY-klops)—One of a race of giants with one huge eye in the center of their forehead. The plural is Cyclopes (sy-kloh-PEEZ).

deities (DEE-ih-teez)—Gods or goddesses.

epic poem (EH-pik POH-um)—A very long poem that describes the adventures of a real or imaginary hero.

fleece—A coat of wool that covers the skin of an animal such as a sheep.

infatuated (in-FAT-choo-ay-ted)—Had a powerful crush on someone; deeply enamored.

immortal (ih-MOR-tul)—A person who cannot die, such as a god.

myths (MITHS)—Stories or beliefs of a culture that help explain their world.

oracle (OR-uh-kul)—A person who tells important information, often about the future.

predestined (pree-DES-tihnd)—Having the outcome already determined.

prophecy (PRAH-feh-see)—A foretelling of an event, revealed by a prophet or seer.

prophesy (PRAH-feh-sy)—To foretell an event.

pyre (PYR)—A pile or heap of wood for burning a dead body.

suitors (SOO-turs)—Traditionally, men who are interested in marrying a woman.